FAITH UNDER FIRE

- New Edition -

REV (DR) TUNDE BOLANTA

Restoration Bible Church and Ministries,

©Tunde Bolanta

First Published 2006
This Edition 2018

ISBN: 978-1-907095-31-3

For more copies, write to:
The Publication Department,
Restoration Bible Church & Ministries, Inc.,
P. O. Box 1485, Kaduna, Nigeria.

This Edition is published by
Winning Faith Publications,
London. UK

Appreciation

My appreciation goes to Winning Faith Publications, London for making this edition available on the global market.

Faith Under Fire

TABLE OF CONTENTS

CHAPTER ONE

THE UNFAILING WORD

Several decades ago, our nation made a new law that required motorist to drive on the right side of the road as opposed to the left side. Some people found this difficult as they were already used to driving on the left for many years while under the British colonial rule.

Motorist with good intentions were often fined because they just forgot which side of the road they were supposed to drive on. The word of God is law ratified by the blood of Jesus and passed in the courts of heaven. It will always work if we obey it. It cannot be challenged, we cannot change it, it changes us.

For as the heavens are higher than the earth, so are my ways higher than your ways, and my thoughts than your thoughts. For as the rain cometh down and the snow from heaven, and returneth not thither, but watereth the earth, and maketh it bring forth and bud that it may give seed to the sower and bread to the eater So shall my word be that goeth forth out of my mouth: it shall not return unto me void, but it shall accomplish that which I please and it shall prosper in the thing whereto I sent it.
Isaiah 55:9-11

For the word of God is quick and powerful, and sharper than any two edged sword, piercing even to the dividing asunder of soul and spirit, and of the joints and marrow, and is a discerner of the thoughts and intents of the heart. Neither is there any creature that is not manifest in his sight: but all things are naked and opened unto the eyes of him with whom we have to do.
Hebrews 4:12-13

Who being the brightness of his glory, and the express image of his person, and upholding all things by the word of his power, when he had by himself purged our sins, sat down on the right hand of the Majesty on high;
Hebrews 1:3

In the beginning was the Word, and the Word was with God, and the Word was God. The same was in the beginning with God. All things were made by him; and without him was not any thing made that was made
John 1:1-3

The word that God speaks is powerful. His word created the universe and nothing can be hidden from His word. The word analyses, sifts and separates. All things are naked and transparent before the word. Whatsoever does not gather with the word scatters. All of God's power is in his word. The universe and all the elements stand and obey the word or fall to the word.

The word of God and God are one. After the word of God has been spoken, there are no arguments. The word of God is law. Jesus said, it is possible for heaven and earth to pass away but the word cannot fail. The word is the source of everything and upholds everything. Should the word fail then, the heavens and the earth must fail because system failure occurs once the heart fails.

God upholds all things by his word. He has also exalted the word above his name. A name is of no value if the words of the bearer cannot be obeyed. A king is of no value if his word has no authority. The word of the king is law where there is authority.

The word of God assumes all the characteristics of God, and will do exactly what He desires. The word of God is God because the Bible says, the word was with God and the word is God.

Most believers have no problem with the

efficacy of God's word but often wonder if the word will have the same effect from their own mouths. God's words are faith- filled and cannot fail. The same faith is available to us, because to every man God has dealt the measure of faith. Jesus enjoined us to have God kind of faith. He wouldn't have said so if it was not possible. The believer in Christ Jesus has a measure of faith, which we can liken to a muscle.

A body builder does not get new muscles apart from the one he got at birth. Though the bulging biceps are noticed, they had always been there. The truth is that, every healthy person has the same capacity to build muscles. Healthy eating habits and exercises are keys to building muscles. The same is applicable to the spiritual realm.

The food that produces energy is the one that we digest. The one that is passed as waste is useless to us. In order to digest food, we chew, swallow and allow the system to do her work.

That energy is used and also stored. We are to attend to the word of God in much the same way, give it our undivided attention, saying it over and over, rolling it in our thought, allowing it to fill our minds and consciousness until we are consumed by it. God's thoughts become ours and our spiritual eyes begin to see His reality more than the situation we are in.

My son, attend to my words; incline thine ear unto my sayings. Let them not depart from thine eyes; keep them in the midst of thine heart. For they are life unto those that find them, and health to all their flesh.
Proverbs 4:20-22

The word used this way will become medicine to all our flesh. The word will work for those who will work it, if we give it the devotion it requires. Much like food, our spirits will digest the food, faith will be there and fear will disappear.

Sometimes we are not aware how much the

word has done in us until the Lord gives us an opportunity to use our faith. A body builder, who eats right and does not practice lifting weights, will develop no muscles. Often times when the devil comes on strong against us, we think God does not really care, but it is simply weight lifting class.

God promised that we shall not be tempted more than we can bear and He will make a way of escape. He also promised to honour and deliver us, this does not remove from the fact that our adversary is real and the test is real and the dangers are apparent. The truth remains; the word must be tested before we can move to a higher grade.

Test of faith
One severe test of faith for me in the early days, was an encounter with witch doctors. They were aggravated at me because I had failed to keep to a ritual tradition of theirs.

This involved dragging a life goat around. The

town was required to be in total darkness. My apartment was the only one lit, so this was; viewed as an affront. I was then surrounded by about seventy persons mainly witch doctors and people from the oracle. They continued to recite incantations commanding me to be blind.

This I saw as both a physical and spiritual attack. The first feeling was that of despair and fear as all the stories of wizardry I had heard, came back to mind. Tales of witches turning into animals to afflict them.

Victims clouded my mind. I felt numb initially wondering what to do. I began to quote Isaiah 54:17, shaking at the same time.

"No weapon that is formed against thee shall prosper and every tongue that shall rise against thee in judgment thou shalt condemn. This is the heritage of the servants of the LORD, and their righteousness is of me, saith the LORD."

Thoughts were going through my mind faster

than you could fire a machine gun, besides I had done a successful crusade in this town with many saved and healed. The devil told me I was going to be humbled and destroyed. As I stood my ground and continued to declare the word of God, fear gave way to confidence and what appeared as lightning was seen around the place where they gathered and they took to their heels.

I was so shocked because I did not know exactly how the Lord would deliver me. The following day the ruler of the town came to me because the town was awash with the story of the lightning. He gave his life to Christ and we planted a church in the town.

When this attack occurred, I did not have time to read my Bible or even Pray, the confusion was what got my attention, by the time I got to the window they were already upset and moments later were using evil incantations commanding me to be blind. The word that delivered me was stored up before the crisis.

Jesus taught that the house must be built before the storms of life come. It must be built on the rock with the foundation deep in the rock.

I have also had stories of other pastors in the same situation that never made it. Did God choose to deliver one and deny the other? It also depends on the amount of word that we put in our minds before the crisis of life.

Why do we go through tests like this one? So that the word is not just head knowledge. Our walk with God is a practical one. We can only be witnesses to the things we have experienced.

As we come through by using the word we can help others who are going through the same thing. How we handle one challenge determines what next we are ready for.

A weight lifter must follow a routine every day in order to prepare for the competition. The same is true of all athletes. Working out daily requires sweat, denial and discomfort but that is the only way to stay in shape. When you work out at a gym, you sweat and it is hard on the flesh. For the word of God to be effective in our lives, the believer must have a lifestyle that is built around the word and fellowship with God.

A person who feeds right, but does no exercise will be fat but not strong. The challenge is not the reason for the strength, but putting the word to use thereby building the muscles is what matters.

Running Over Cup

Thou preparest a table before me in the presence of mine enemies thou anointest my head with oil; my cup runneth over.
Psalms 23:5

O generation of vipers, how can ye being evil, speak good things? for out of the abundance of the heart the mouth speaketh. A good man out of the good treasure of the heart bringeth forth

good things: and an evil man out of the evil treasure bringeth forth evil things.
Matthew 12:34-35

This book of the law shall not depart out of thy mouth; but thou shalt meditate therein day and night, that thou mayest observe to do according to all that is written therein: forthen thou shalt make thy way prosperous and then thou shalt have good success.
Joshua 1:8

One will wonder why a cup must be filled before it runs over. A cup that is full has limited impact. A cup that runs over affects the environment. When the Psalmist wrote 'my cup runneth over' he was echoing what was in the mind of God.

Jesus said, 'out of the abundance of the heart the mouth speaketh1. What is in one's heart in abundance will come out and affect the person's life.

The word has to abide in us to a level that we

are sure we have enough, supplied in excess. For example, a person whose account is in excess of a hundred million dollars is not afraid to make withdrawals for a few hundred dollars. We spend faith the way we spend money, the fact that you put money in your account last month, does not mean you still have enough. The more you use, the more you need otherwise your upkeep will result in your downfall.

The word must dwell in us richly. Colossians 3 :16-17 it must overflow and be in abundance to have real impact. Recently in Denmark, I was invited by a friend to have dinner. After the meal and fellowship, they shared something very encouraging with me.

Six years ago, they struggled to have a child but were not given any hope medically. They then approached me for prayers. I shared with them on redemption and gave them scriptures to meditate on. She still had the paper with my handwriting on. They said, they meditated and confessed this faithfully and the Lord blessed them, with a beautiful baby girl who sat with us at the table.

I remembered another situation. I prayed for a woman in a wheelchair who leapt out of the chair but because I had my eyes closed, I did not realize what happened until the noise from the congregation attracted me. I then realized, that God had done a notable miracle, we rejoiced and I had fun, as she pushed me around in her chair.

This excitement soon dissipated because another woman in a wheel chair next to her was disappointed as nothing visible happened in her case. People stood on chairs expecting something to happen probably as dramatic as the other lady's.

The Lord spoke to me to share healing scriptures with her. I gave her many of these, and directed she spend an hour morning, afternoon, and night, on these scriptures. The following year, I was ministering in another place and a woman walked towards me with her daughter.

She testified that she had followed the instructions religiously, her fear disappeared and she improved gradually until she got out of her chair!

The interesting thing about this is that, in both cases, they received by simply filling their heart with The Word' until it overflowed. This is a way you receive all the time, because, the Word is already anointed. Once the word gets into the heart and overflows, it would affect us and change whatever needs changing.

The word made everything and everything is subject to it as we saw in the earlier chapter. The most important thing is to get the word in every situation. When God wanted to change the world, he sent Jesus-the word, into the darkness to change it. John I: I-5. In the beginning God spoke his word into the darkness.

When my daughter was conceived it was a challenge because the pregnancy was threatened with miscarriage as there was continual bleeding. We were out on a mission trip preaching every night and it seemed in the natural that the pregnancy would be lost at any time.

You just have to stand and ignore the sense evidence. The bleeding was non- stop for months but we kept our confession. You can only do that, if you stay in the overflow. In a situation like this, you are using your faith, like a car using petrol you must refill.

The physical evidence was definitely negative. It was easy to have given up, going by the physical evidence. To stay on top of the situation, we needed to keep the word in our mouths and before our eyes according to

Proverbs 4:20-22 which states:

My son, attend to my words; incline thine ear

onto my sayings. Lei them not depart from thine eyes; keep them in the midst of thine heart. For they are life unto those that find them, and health to all their flesh.

The psalmist wrote about a running over cup, a Cup that does not only have water inside, but outside. In the battles of life, we need to be fortified on the inside and on the outside.

A running over cup cannot be dry. When push comes to shove, and natural evidence is contrary, the believer needs to have his cup running over with the word. This does not happen by paying lip service to the word.

There is no overdose with the word, only overflow. In a similar manner that the alcoholic keeps drinking until he is oblivious of his natural circumstances the believer must keep feeding on the word until it becomes more real than the challenges.

It could mean waking up three times to read the

same scripture over and over, you may need to paste scriptures on your refrigerator, you must do whatever you need to do, to keep the word going in and out of you.

CHAPTER TWO

FAITH IS AN ACT

A short while after the September 11 crisis I travelled to the U.S. The fear was palpable. People were looking at each other with suspicion. Any one that looked or acted differently was suspect.

Of course, thoughts were going through my head that something could go wrong. When the Bible, says, fear not, it is not denying the danger but it is insisting on a higher law in the face of danger.

Danger occurs when there is no higher

intervention. A plane with its heavy weight is a dangerous thing to get on without the law of aerodynamics it would not take off from the runway. Every dangerous challenge need not be feared because there is a higher law in the word of God. Although your pulse may race and there may be palpitations just do it afraid.

The account of Jesus when he was invited to Jairus' house is a good example of how to deal with fear. While Jesus was on his way to Jairus house news reached him that his daughter had died Jesus turned to him and said 'fear not only believe'.

The amplified Bible says, 'overhearing but ignoring what they said, Jesus said to the ruler of the synagogue. Do not be seized with alarm and struck with fear; only keep on believing Mark 5:36 (amplified).

This is Jesus' instruction on how to deal with fear. He knew the ruler was naturally afraid, he was not asking him to deny his feelings, but just as Jesus heard the report and ignored it, he asked him to do the same. In other words when there is a higher law superseding the lower law of death we can focus our mind on God and ignore the feelings of fear in the natural. Jairus kept silent.

He did not reply the messenger who broke the news to him he was silent. His faith was expressed in his silence, perhaps if he had talked he would have said the wrong thing-I'm sure his head gave him trouble as anyone's head would in that situation.

There is therefore now no condemnation to them which are in Christ Jesus, who walk not after the flesh, but after the Spirit. For the law of the Spirit of life in Christ Jesus hath made me free from the law of sin and death.
Romans 8:1-2

And they heard the voice of the LORD God walking in the garden in the cool of the day: and Adam and his wife hid themselves from the presence of the LORD God amongst the trees of the garden. And the LORD God called unto Adam, and said unto him. Where art thou? And he said I heard thy voice in the garden, and I was afraid because I was naked; and I hid myself. **Genesis 3:8-10**

And when the disciples saw him walking on the sea, they were troubled saying. It is a spirit; and they cried out for fear. But straightway Jesus spake unto them, saying Be of good cheer it is I; be not afraid And Peter answered him and said Lord, if it be thou, bid me come unto thee on the water.

And he said Come, And when Peter was come down out of the ship, he walked on the water, to go to Jesus. But when he saw the wind boisterous, he was afraid and beginning to sink he cried saying Lord, save me. And immediately Jesus stretched forth his hand, and caught him, and said unto him, O thou of little faith, wherefore didst thou doubt And when they were come into the ship, the wind ceased

Then they that we in the ship came and worshipped him, saying Of a truth thou art the Son of God. **Mathew 14:26-33**

The law of the Spirit of life operates by faith while the law of sin and death operates by fear. The latter was evident in the Garden of Eden because immediately Adam sinned he was afraid of the presence of God.

Fear is a signal that sin and Satan are present because perfect love or the love of God cast out fear. Fear is opposite of faith. When present, faith will not operate. The story of Peter is an apt example of what fear does to faith. Peter began to walk on water in response to the word of Jesus 'come'.

This four-letter word from the lips of the master was enough to sustain Peter on water irrespective of the natural circumstances. Peter began to pay attention to the natural circumstances and he began to sink. Naturally, you cannot walk on water.

The wind had nothing to do with his ability to walk on water. He would have sunk on a perfectly still night; his weight would have sunk him. The only enabler is the word. The moment he took his eyes off that word which was still in force he began to sink. The word is designed to change natural circumstances. The size of the problem notwithstanding, without wind, Peter could not have walked on water his attention to the natural cost him his victory.

No Venom No Sting

And the LORD said unto Moses, Make thee a fiery serpent, and set it upon a pole: and it shall come to pass, that every one that is bitten when he looketh upon it, shall live. **Numbers 21:8**

And Moses made a serpent of brass, and put it upon a pole, and it came to pass, that if a serpent had bitten any man, when he beheld the serpent of brass, he lived. **Numbers 21:9**

And as Moses lifted up the serpent in the

wilderness, even so must the Son of man be lifted up. **John 3:14**

And I, if I be lifted up from the earth, will draw oil men unto me. **John 12:32**

Christ hath redeemed us from the curse of the law, being made a curse for us: for it is written Cursed is everyone that hangeth on a tree: **Galatians 3:13**

Fear has been rightly described as false evidence appearing real comparable with a mirage on a hot and sunny day, when it is approached it disappears. When the children of Israel sinned against God and were bitten by serpents, God instructed Moses to make a bronze serpent and whosoever looked upon it shall be healed.

The serpent that bit them had venom but the serpent they looked upon had no venom. The Lord Jesus referring to this later in the gospel said, just as the serpent was lifted up in the wilderness and those who looked on it were healed, when he is lifted on the cross, through his death, burial, and resurrection, those who will look upon him shall also be set free.

The serpent represented the curse of sin and its attendant penalties such as sicknesses, weaknesses, distresses, fears, destructions, lack, death and all pertaining to the devil but Jesus came and crushed the head of the devil meaning there is no longer venom there.

He became a curse for us when we look on him now we see him as our curse bearer. We view all curses buried with him. In him the venom of the curses was crushed. The believer can say, oh death where is your sting because it has been crushed in Christ.

You can safely handle a snake that has no venom. The Lord Jesus emasculated the devil the cross. This reminds of the pranks some children once played while we were in elementary school.

They would put a plastic snake on the Mathematics teacher's chair before her lesson. When she came in, one of the pupils would shout from the back of the classroom pointing to her chair just as she entered in. This would send her rushing out of the class. She never knew it was a plastic snake. No venom so the fear of the unknown has kept many believers in bondage.

The word says you will know the truth and the truth shall set you free. I remember another situation with an ex-service man, who had a wooden gun, which he used to extract taxes from a colony of lepers. The gun was well painted and with it he terrorized the people. Someone told them the gun was not real and they decided to get their revenge.

One early morning they laid siege at his door waiting for him. When he failed to show up they broke down the door. He was actually surprised at the audacity they had to come into his room, he threatened to shoot and the lepers told him to go ahead.

They ascended on him with many blows injuring him severely in the process and he was hospitalized. The Bible says the enemy holds people in bondage all their lives because of fear. The believer can look any situation in the face and say 'no venom no fear', from Cancers to Aids, to deliverance from danger of all types, are part of our redemption see

Bless the LORD, O my soul: and all that is within me, bless his holy name. Bless the LORD, Omy soul, and forget not all his benefits: Who forgiveth all thine iniquities; who healeth all thy diseases; Who redeemeth thy life from destruction; who crowneth thee with loving-kindness and tender mercies; Who satisfieth thy mouth with good things; so that thy youth is renewed like the eagle's.
Psalm103:1-5.

In the Amplified translation it states in part, in John 16:33, *"I have denied it power to harm you".* Jesus was teaching here that the tribulations of life may come but they have been denied power to hurt us because, he already took the venom. Imagine for a moment that someone had a gun to your head in which there are no bullets in it. That is exactly what the devil does.

The fear of diseases, destruction, poverty and whatsoever he throws at the believer. The bullets were absorbed on the cross and the gun to your head is only a threat

Forasmuch then as the children are partakers of flesh and blood, he also himself likewise took part of the same; that through death he might destroy him that had the power of death, that is the devil; And deliver them who through fear of death were all their lifetime subject to bondage. **Hebrews 2:14-15**

Believers are spiritual beings, living in the natural, sustained by the word. Natural challenges should have no control over us because; the law of God's word is infallible, proven by many generations. This word formed the heaven and the earth, it sustained Noah during the flood, rose as the flood rose, secured a destiny for Abraham who left home for nowhere, delivered Joseph from treachery, delivered Israel from the red sea, conquered the promise land for them.

This word delivered Daniel from the lion's den, quenched the flames of fire for the three Hebrew children, took on flesh and produced the Messiah, turned water into wine, gave the Wind their sight, raised the Lord Jesus from the dead. It has never been known to fail; it works the same, no margin for error.

The Scriptures record that every time God comes on the scene he says fear not, fear is the opposite of faith. These two are opposed to each other and cannot operate together.

Why do believers experience the sensation of fear, when they are walking in faith? When the scriptures say fear not, it means you may experience the sensation of fear; such as sweaty palm, quickened pulse, panic, rush of blood to your head but, don't succumb to it, it is an attack.

A friend who received a pilot license some years ago, wanted to take me flying. I was naturally excited. The whole idea was, have some fun and pray over his nation. We strapped on in the cockpit.

The small aircraft taxied and took off. It was a very good day for flying, the sky was clear, my friend was really excited; he explained procedures to me and tried to show me certain landmarks.

He proceeded to have some demonstrations perhaps, things he did with his instructor but my ordeal began. He took certain turns; some moves that seemed to me like flipping the aircraft. I shouted Jesus! At the same time binding the devil, I did not do much praying for his country I was praying to get down safely.

At a point, he wanted to fly low enough over his mother's kitchen, so she could see him and the butterflies in my stomach were really taking off. While he was going to land, things were going really fast.

Looking out the window I thought he was going in too quickly. He told me to keep my eyes on the meter because he was coming in at the right speed. I share this experience because, it demonstrates that you become afraid; when you are not sure of the law you are operating on.

My friend laughed all the way enjoying himself. He knew the laws. The word of God says you shall know the truth, and the truth shall set you free. Fear may fill your mind but you can act against your fear when you refuse to focus on the natural.

You always act on something either your fear

or your faith. There is no middle ground. Acting on your faith releases the power of God.

Raised to Life
While writing this chapter I had a visitor with whom we had a hair-raising experience. Talk about panic, fear and drama we had all of it, but victory came when the word of God was acted upon.

Our ministry team was travelling for an outreach in another city. The passenger vehicle was loaded with people and instruments and we were running late. I travelled in another car and departed a little over an hour after the team set out.

The passenger vehicle was involved in an accident somersaulting several times it landed in a ditch. Many sustained injuries and our Evangelist was killed. When I arrived at the scene there was pandemonium, team members were looking for transportation to take injured persons to hospital.

The body of the Evangelist had been conveyed to the side of the road from the bush lifeless. People were screaming and there was confusion. We surrounded the body and I asked everyone to pray.

While praying, I had a voice three times. It said you can call him back. I dismissed it thinking it must be the devil. But then I reckoned it was better to obey even though my head did not agree. When I called his name, and commanded as I was instructed; Instantly, he stirred and opened his eyes! He was very upset, he recounted being in a far better place!

Faith not acted upon will not bring results. Faith is an act. If you don't release what you believe through words and action the power will not manifest.

Paul was preaching at Lystra, there was a man lame from his mother's womb. He heard the word faith came into his heart, but there was no healing until Paul shouted and told him to get up. He was healed. Without acting on what he believed he would have received nothing. Faith that says nothing and does nothing receives nothing. Acts 14:8-10

Feelings are ways our senses speak to us. In this particular situation, the natural feeling was one of fear but you can have faith in your heart with fear in your head because your heart is where the presence of God is; and your feelings only remind you that you are still in the natural.

When you focus on your feelings in the case of healing, your feelings may be worse after you pray and believe, you need to establish a point where you believe.

You come to a place where you accept the word as your final authority, and from that point you are giving thanks for the answer. Peter's point of belief was when he stepped out in faith. If he did not believe he would have sat back with the others in the boat. The point of belief is when you start acting against your fear. The Bible says Abraham was not weak in faith, but was giving glory to God.

This point is established when you have put the word in you to a degree where you are ready to act on the word. Faith is a verb an active word. When you are unable to act on what you claim to believe, you are not in faith.

Acting on the word, should never be presumptuous that is why you need to spend time in the word until, your confidence in acting on it comes from the word alone and not feelings.

Hope is a good waiter, it puts the answer in the future: one day something is going to happen. Faith says I have it now in the spirit, and the manifestation, is on the way, and acting like I have the answer in the natural, no sadness, no worries, no moodiness am joyful.

CHAPTER THREE

CASTING YOUR CARES

I read the story of a woman who kept going to her doctor with a complaint that she suspected she had cancer. The doctor could find not trace of cancer but after fifteen years or so cancer showed up in her body and she died.

She feared cancer, kept calling cancer and cancer answered and killed her. What we fear always show up in our words and eventually in our lives. Fear like a telephone exchange will respond.

There are different telecommunication

networks. Ignorance about the network you are dialling does not stop you from getting an answer. Another name for worry is fear. The root cause of every anxiety is fear that something bad may happen.

Humble yourselves therefore under the mighty hand of God, that he may exalt you in due time: Casting all your care upon him; for he care for you. **1 Peter 5:6-7**

Be careful for nothing; but in everything by prayer and supplication with thanksgiving let your requests be made known unto God. And the peace of God, which passeth all understanding, shall keep your hearts and minds through Christ Jesus. **Philippians 4:6-7**

Therefore I say unto you, Take no thought for your life, what ye shall eat or what ye shall drink nor yet for your body, what ye shall put on Is not the life more than meat, and the body than raiment? Behold the fowls of the air: for they sow not, neither do they reap nor gather into barns; yet your heavenly Father feedeth them. Are ye not much better than they? Which of you by taking thought can add one cubit unto his stature? And why take ye thought for raiment? Consider the lilies of the field, how they grow they toil not, neither do they spin And yet I say unto you.

That even Solomon in all his glory was not arrayed like one of these. Wherefore, if God so clothe the grass   of the   field, which to day is and tomorrow is cast into the oven, shall he not much more clothe you, O ye of little faith? Therefore take no thought saying What shall we eat or, What shall we drink or. Wherewithal shall we be clothed For after all these things do the Gentiles seek for your heavenly Father knoweth that ye have need of all these things.

But seek ye first the kingdom of God, and his righteousness; and all these things shall be added unto you. Take therefore no thought for the morrow: for the morrow shall take thought for the things of itself. Sufficient unto the day is

the evil thereof.
Mathew 6:25-34

Worry is a sin. One of the biggest battles you need to fight in order for faith to work is to win over worry. It is a manifestation of the spirit of fear, a subtle thing. It disguises itself in reason.

You always have enough logical reasons to worry. Worry tries to solve tomorrow's problems by taking them on board today. But Jesus said everyday has its own trouble. He was saying in other words do not weigh yourself down about tomorrow because, God gives you grace for one day at a time.

The folly of worrying is that: worry does not change the situation, it only changes you. It increases your stress level, it creates other physical problems from headaches to high blood pressure, psychosomatic disorders and the list is endless.

Why pay with your health for a situation you

don't like; that amounts to double torment. Worry also calls God a liar and questions his word and wisdom. Some scriptures come to mind, Romans 8:26-28 God says He can work out the worst situation for your good if you love him.

I am reminded of four women who appeared in the lineage of Christ: Rahab, Tamar, Bathsheba, Ruth. Rahab was the harlot of Jericho, Tamar committed incest with her father in-law, Ruth was the Moabite woman whose ancestors were products of incest between Lot and his daughters but they chose to love God despite their history and God turned their future around.

Likewise the Spirit also helpeth our infirmities: for we know not what we should pray for as we ought but the Spirit itself maketh intercession for us with groanings which cannot be uttered. And he that searcheth the hearts knoweth what is the mind of the Spirit, because he maketh intercession for the saints according to the will of God. And we know that all things work together for good to them that love God, to them who are the called according to his purpose. **Romans 8:26-28**

In righteousness shalt thou be established thou shalt be far from oppression; for thou shalt not fear and from terror; for it shall not come near thee. Behold, they shall surely gather together but not by me: whosoever shall gather together against thee shall fall for thy sake. Behold, I have created the smith that bloweth the coals in the fire, and that bringeth forth an instrument for his work; and I have created the waster to destroy No weapon that is formed against thee shall prosper and every tongue that shall rise against thee in judgment thou shalt condemn. This is the heritage of the servants of the LORD, and their righteousness is of me, saith the LORD. **Isaiah 54:14-17**

Because he hath set his love upon me, therefore will I deliver him: I will set him on high because he hath known my name. He shall call

upon me, and I will answer him: I will be with him in trouble; I will deliver him,and honour him.
Psalms 91:14-15

Worry stops your prayer from working because we are required to cast our cares before we pray. Praying without releasing our care is like running with a limp. Philippians 4:6-7 says ...do not fret or have anxiety about anything, which means no exception. God has also promised to deliver us from trouble and honour us.

In Isaiah 54:14-16, Psalm 91:15-16, he said no weapon formed against us prospers because he created the world and has authority over every weapon of destruction. They may destroy others but in the day they were formed they were instructed not to touch those who belong to God they understand the blood line of the Lord Jesus the blood of atonement that continually speaks deliverance over the children of God.

Daniel had every reason to be worried going

into a lion's den but he went knowing God would deliver him, the animals   recognized that   they   could   not consume this man. The same is true in your situation. You may be attacked but will not be consumed what makes this to work is the power of God's word producing a rest.

Worry is a waste of time because it never changes your situation but instead stops the flow of God's power into the situation. When Moses came to the Red Sea with the host of Pharaoh behind and the sea in front they were hedged in, God told him to go forward he showed his faith and defeated his worry and fear by moving.

Worry stops all forward movements, you are unable to think, unproductive. The only way you can show you have practically defeated worry is that you are moving in the direction of your purpose.

Philippians 4:6-7 also speaks of thanksgiving,

we are not thanking God for evil or the attack but we are thanking him because he is at work in the situation, he is at work to deliver, he is at work to make us more like Christ, by perfecting our character.

You cannot loose. In rural Africa where one soccer ball may be all a group in a community have, to play with the boy who owns the ball is king. The boy who owns the ball never losses out, to send him home means he picks up his ball and the game ends, so he ends up playing till he is tired. The same is true for the child of God.

God is able and willing to turn situations in our favour because the psalmist says 'the earth is the Lord's and the fullness thereof and the people that dwell therein'.

Thanksgiving is voicing out your praise such as 'I am worry free because God is working everything out for my good, every weapon against me has failed, I am delivered and honoured out of this situation'. It is a sacrifice because your natural situation may not have improved while you are doing this.

I am the true vine, and my Father is the husbandman. Every branch in me that beareth not fruit he taketh away and every branch that beareth fruit, he purgeth it, that it may bring forth more fruit. Now ye are clean through the word which I have spoken unto you. Abide in me, and I in you. As the branch cannot bear fruit of itself, except it abide in the vine; no more can ye, except ye abide in me. I am the vine, ye are the branches: He that abideth in me, and I in him, the same bringeth forth much fruit: for without me ye can do nothing.
John 15:1-5

You don't need to worry because Jesus said in the above passage that he is the vine we are the branches and our heavenly Father is the husbandman.

What this implies literarily is that our lives are

sustained by God and as long as we remain in fellowship with Jesus the vine, we may seem weak and unable to stand on our own but we are held up by the vine.

The branch of a tree may dangle from the trunk but big roots sustain it. The believer is rooted in God Almighty. Our lives are rooted in Christ and Christ in God.

God not the devil, is the husbandman or vinedresser, this means whatever happens, God is in control because the garden is his, not the devils, Satan may attack us but he is not our Lord and we are not planted in his garden therefore whatever happens he must back off.

The owner of the garden takes full responsibility for the life, provision, and destiny of the garden. He is more concerned about the garden because the garden is a reflection of him. The garden's reputation is a reflection of him, we can therefore rest knowing that, the husbandman is mindful of us as a gardener is mindful of his garden.

On the contrary, a father who does more for his family without them asking and is prompt in meeting their needs will not be bombarded with reminder notes and looks but with appreciation cards. Thanksgiving is thanking God for what he has done and what he is going to do.

CHAPTER FOUR

ABOUNDING IN THANKSGIVING

A sailor that forgets certain critical details would endanger the life of everyone on board. He must not forget to lower the sails or to let down the anchor. He must not neglect to tie knots well while mooring the ship to the dock.

In the walk of faith thanksgiving is a critical element we cannot live without. Seeking first the kingdom of God is actually living in the kingdom and learning how it works.

A father is famous for breaking promises to his children if they send him weekly reminders of a favour he has promised because the children are used to his lies.

Rejoice in the Lord always: and again I say Rejoice Let your moderation be known unto all men. The Lord is at hand. Be careful for nothing; but in every thing by prayer and supplication with thanksgiving let your requests be made known unto God. And the peace of God, which passeth all understanding, shall keep your hearts and minds through Christ Jesus. **Philippians 4:4-7**

Abide in me, and I in you. As the branch cannot bear fruit of itself, except it abide in the vine; no more can ye, except ye abide in me. I am the vine, ye are the branches: He that abideth in me, and I in him, the same bringeth forth much fruit: for without me ye can do nothing. If a man abides not in me, he is cast forth as a branch, and is withered and men gather them, and cast them into the fire, and they are burned. If ye abide in me, and my words abide in you, ye shall ask what ye will and it shall be done unto you. Herein is my Father glorified that ye bear much fruit; so shall ye be my disciples. As the Father hath loved me, so have I loved you: continue ye in my love. If ye keep my commandments, ye shall abide in my love; even as I have. **John 15:4-10**

The Apostle Paul makes it clear that thanksgiving is essential if faith will produce. Many times in the midst of crisis the believer has done all he knows to do and there is no breakthrough he needs to use the weapon of praise.

Paul writes this with the experience of a veteran who is skillful in the use of the weapon of praise, a man who was beaten up in prison but chose praise over grumbling and complaining, in the mid night of the crisis. History records that he was in prison when he wrote to the Philippians and commanded them to rejoice always.

Giving thanks is the will of God in all situations

because every challenge is another avenue to prove his faithfulness. Nothing should stress us because we are confident in our relationship with the father.

Giving thanks always for all things unto God and the Father in the name of our Lord Jesus Christ; **Ephesians 5:20**

Giving thanks unto the Father, which hath made us meet to be partakers of the inheritance of the saints in light.
Colossians 1:12

Faith is not mechanical, real faith is based on relationship. Supposing a man, you do not know promises a million dollars you would wonder about his ability to come up with that sum on the set day. You may hesitate going to the bank with the cheque fearing that things won't work out.

If you know the man well and you know he has the capacity to have that amount in his account you would be a bit relieved but not totally. You would like to know if he was a giver by nature, and who else has benefited from his generosity?

You would then ask another question why would he want to help me? His character and your relationship with him would help you to trust his word or otherwise. In another place Paul says I know whom I have believed in, we are grafted into the vine we are one with him, nothing, absolutely nothing, can separate us.

For the which cause I also suffer these things: nevertheless I am not ashamed for I know whom I have believed and am persuaded that he is able to keep that which I have committed unto him against that day.
2 Timothy 1:12

His relationship with the Lord keeps him steady. Two men motioned to a child to jump off a high table into their waiting hands, the first man a guest at their home when he requested the child to leap into his waiting arms the child burst into tears and cried.

The child's father repeated the same request and the child jumped into the father's waiting arms. What made the difference? The child knew the father would be there to catch him as for the stranger he was not so sure. This is why Jesus emphasized that my sheep know my voice and the voice of a stranger they would not hear.

Knowing him is an essential part of faith otherwise you would only repeat what others have told you about him. Knowing him comes through intimacy. Fellowshipping with him in prayer, worship and the word builds intimacy.

CHAPTER FIVE

ADD TO YOUR FAITH CHARACTER

Faith will not be developed at the expense of the fruit of the spirit: which is our Christian character. Let us imagine for a moment the heir to the greatest monarchy on the earth ascends the throne after the glorious reign and exit of his father but has none of his noble character.

He immediately starts enjoying all of the riches, advantage and comfort of that office by virtue of his birth and position but he is foul mouthed temperate, immoral, immodest and vile. He would be a disgrace to the throne. If the father knew this aspect of him before leaving he would do everything to make sure that his character developed alongside his inheritance.

This explains why the Lord works both character and inheritance at the same time because we represent him here. There is nothing that we need that is not already ours in Christ but you don't give a loaded gun to a toddler. He may kill you!

According as his divine power hath given unto us all things that pertain unto life and godliness, through the knowledge of him that hath called us to glory and virtue: Whereby are given unto us exceeding great and precious promises: that by these ye might be partakers of the divine nature, having escaped the corruption that is in the world through lust. And beside this, giving all diligence, add to your faith virtue; and to virtue knowledge; And to knowledge temperance; and to temperance patience; and to patience godliness; And to godliness brotherly kindness; and to brotherly kindness charity. For if these things be in you, and abound they make you that ye shall neither be barren nor unfruitful in the knowledge of our Lord Jesus Christ. But he that lacketh these things is blind, and cannot see afar off and hath forgotten that he was purged from his old sins. Wherefore the rather, brethren, give diligence to make your calling and election sure: for if ye do these things, ye shall never fall.

2 Timothy 3:1-10

My brethren, count it all joy when ye fall into divers temptations; Knowing this, that the trying of your faith worketh patience. But let patience have her perfect work, that ye may be perfect and entire, wanting nothing.

James 1:2-4

And Jesus answering saith unto them, Have faith in God. For verily I say unto you, That whosoever shall say unto this mountain, Be thou removed and be thou cast into the sea; and shall not doubt in his heart, but shall believe that those things which he saith shall

come to pass he shall have whatsoever he saith Therefore I say unto you. What things soever ye desire when ye pray believe that ye receive them, and ye shall have them.
Mark 11:22-24

And this is the confidence that we have in him, that, if we ask any thing according to his will, he heareth us. **1 John 5:14**

What happens after you have meditated on the word, and were confident that, what you asked you received when you prayed, and there is a delay. Patience must come to play. Patience like all the other fruits of the spirit is a fruit not a gift. It takes time for fruits to grow: growth is a process. God wants the fruits of the spirit to mature in our lives.

The fruit shows our character; that is why Paul writing to Timothy says, we must add certain things; Christ-like character, temperance, patience, godliness, et cetera to our faith in order for it to work effectively. God is always ensuring that, before the manifestation of the answer, you manifest some fruit.

In the case of healing, which you receive by believing the word, you are also drawn into intimacy with God as you are relying on his word, in the face of contradictory physical evidence. The Holy Spirit your helper may start showing you areas of your love walk where you need to make changes.

The Apostle James writes about counting it all joy when, you fall into divers temptation and trials. How do you do that when someone has been ugly, or, they have made up untrue stories about you or have defrauded you?

The reason you count it joy is that, the trial is producing the fruit of patience. He said the trial of your faith works patience. So, count it all joy. James is saying, don't focus on the discomfort; focus on the fruit that the Holy Spirit, is helping you grow in your life. True, God is not the one trying to destroy, rob, and kill you but as you use the word, character development is the by-product of the trial.

In situations of test you also gather needed experience that will help you, stand against similar challenges in the future. The Amplified Bible says when patience has perfected its work we become people 'fully developed'. Jesus told us, in this world, there would be test and trials.

You can't pray them off or confess them away. They will come but you have already overcome, when you pass through character development.

A wife can read her husband a recipe book but that does not mean she can cook the menu. The Bible is a recipe book of how to live but God wants to see you live it.

All your spiritual muscles are in place because, you are born of God but they are not developed. All the fruits of the Spirit are in place but not developed. The challenges and the tests put pressure on that fruit to come forth. Sometimes you go through certain situations over and over again; it is either the character lesson is not learnt, or the fruit needs be stronger.

God is not the one sending sickness or poverty your way because, Jesus bore those. But it is still a challenge when you go through such situations and you just strengthen the fruit of patience and any other, the Lord wants to develop in that situation, while you resist sin, sickness, poverty, and destruction.

If you play dead, you develop nothing. The pressure comes and you push off the weight by your faith, and, the fruit of the spirit helping you to stay strong.

But the fruit of the Spirit is love, joy, peace, longsuffering, gentleness, goodness, faith. Meekness, temperance: against such there is no law. And they that are Christ's have crucified the flesh with the affections and lusts.

If we live in the Spirit, let us also walk in the Spirit. Let us not be desirous of vain glory, provoking one another, envying one another. Galatians 5:22-26

Charity suffereth long and is kind charity envieth not; charity vaunteth not itself is not puffed up Doth not behave itself unseemly seeketh not her own, is not easily provoked thinketh no evil: Rejoiceth not in iniquity, but rejoiceth in the truth; Beareth all things, believeth all things, hopeth all things, endureth all things. Charity never faileth but whether there be prophecies, they shall fail whether there be tongues, they shall cease whether there be knowledge, it shall vanish away.
1 Corinthians 13:4-8

For in Jesus Christ neither circumcision availeth anything, nor uncircumcision; but faith which worketh by love.
Galatians 5:6b

The fruit of the spirit is summarized in love. The amplified puts love in more practical detail.

"Love endures long and is patient and kind; love never is envious nor boils over with jealousy, is not boastful or vainglorious, does not display itself haughtily. It is not conceited (arrogant and inflated with pride); it is not rude (unmannerly) and does not act unbecomingly. Love (God's love in us) does not insist on its own rights or its own way, for it is not self-seeking; it is not touchy or fretful or resentful; it takes no account of the evil done to it [it pays no attention to a suffered wrong]. It does not rejoice at injustice and unrighteousness, but rejoices when right and truth prevail. Love bears up under anything and everything that comes, is ever ready to believe the best of every person, its hopes are fadeless under all circumstances, and it endures everything [without weakening]. Love never fails [never fades out or becomes obsolete or comes to an end..." (AMP) **1 Corinthians 13:4-8a**

A careful reading of the above in the amplified translation drives home the truth; the more we walk in love, the more we become like Jesus. Not only when people are ugly, or mean spirited, but, when we trust God, for answers in different areas of our lives.

Walking in love is the only way of victory. No matter how stretched we are, we can't loose because, God is love. The love walk ensures that, we walk in all the fruit of the spirit deposited in us, at the new birth because; we are partakers of the divine nature.

Strife puts paid to your faith because, where there is strife, there is confusion and, every evil work and faith, which works by love, will fail.

Jacob's transformation is a good example of faith developed alongside the character of God. We know Jacob to be a man who had great promises made to him although he was a cheat who stole both the birth right, and the blessings from his brother Esau. God made sure that, he prospered and the promises were fulfilled progressively in his life. Godly character was developed alongside. Faith and the fruit is God's ideal. Jacob prayed after running from his brother, he left home with a stick, but came back rich, because of the blessing that was upon him. But, God did not bless him at the expense of his character.

The Eagle is the Christian ideally considered. When the eagle lays her egg on some craggy heights, she delights in bringing delectable meat portions, which is every eaglets dream. The eaglet does not need to pray for this.

The mother just brings them in. After a while the mother begins to scatter the nest, yanking the eaglet out of the nest. The eaglet wonders what has gone wrong with her mother and if the party was coming to an end.

The same situation is true of the believers' life. As a very young believer, God shows us his majesty, and, his love. Even when we pray wrong prayers, using scriptures out of context, he still answers. Even when we have been hopelessly unfaithful, he just stood strong for us but a time comes in our lives like the eaglet when we must learn to fly.

The eaglet is yanked out of the nest, backed by the mother, she feels comfortable for a while, only for the mother to dump her a thousand feet in the air and she thinks she would not make it and, just about the time she is about to crash, the mother picks her up.

Previously, having learnt about the mother's ability to provide in the nest, now she is learning it in a life and death situation. This process is repeated severally, and she begins to flap her wings, and learns to fly.

The mother has answered her prayers for food by teaching her to fly, training her to confront her fear of falling, learning to hunt and above all becoming like the mother in character. God meeting our needs is as important as learning to become more like him.

God answered Jacob's prayers and did more than he asked for, but He at the same time trained him in godliness. Character is the by product of faith. If you do not become more like God as you walk in faith then, there has been a short cut, you are simply faking it and no matter how glorious it would not last.

Let's take a cursory look at Jacob's life from the following scriptural passages:

And he said Is not he rightly named Jacob? For he hath supplanted me these two times: he took away my birthright; and, behold, now he hath taken away my blessing. And he said Hast thou not reserved a blessing for me? And Isaac answered and said unto Esau, Behold, I have made him thy lord, and all his brethren have I given to him for servants; and with corn and wine have I sustained him: and what shall I do now unto thee, my son? And Esau said unto his father, Hast thou but one blessing, my father?

bless me, even me also, O my father. And Esau lifted up his voice, and wept
Genesis 27:37-38

And he lighted upon a certain place, and tarried there all night because the sun was set and he took of the stones of that place, and put them for his pillows, and lay down in that place to sleep And he dreamed and behold a ladder set up on the earth, and the top of it reached to heaven: and behold the angels of God ascending and descending on it. And, behold, the LORD stood above it, and said I am the LORD God of Abraham thy father, and the God of Isaac: the land whereon thou liest to thee will I give it and to thy seed; And thy seed shall be as the dust of the earth, and thou shalt spread abroad to the west, and to the east, and to the north, and to the south: and in thee and in thy seed shall all the families of the earth be blessed And, behold, I am with thee, and will keep thee in all places whither thou goest and will bring thee again into this land; for I will not leave thee, until I have done that which I have spoken to thee of. And Jacob awaked out of his sleep, and he said Surely the LORD is in this place; and I knew it not. And he was afraid and said How dreadful is this place! this is none other but the house of God, and this is the gate of heaven. And Jacob rose up early in the morning, and took the stone that he had put for his pillows, and set it up for a pillar. and poured oil upon the top of it. And he called the name of that place Bethel: but the name of that city was called luz at the tint. And Jacob vowed a vow, saying If God will be with me, and will keep me in this way that I go and will give me bread to eat and raiment to put on So that I come again to my father's house in peace; then shall the LORD be my God: And this stone, which I have set for a pillar, shall be God's house: and of all that thou shalt give me / will surely give the tenth unto thee.

Genesis 28:11-22

And Jacob was wroth and chode with Laban: and Jacob answered and said to iaban, What is my trespass? what is my sin, that thou hast so hotly pursued after me? Whereas thou hast searched all my stuff, what hast thou found of all thy household stuff? set it here before my brethren and thy brethren, that they may judge betwixt us both.

This twenty years have I been with thee; thy ewes and thy she goats have not cast their young and the rams of thy flock have I not eaten That which was torn of beasts I brought not unto thee; I bare the loss of it; of my hand didst thou require it whether stolen by day, or stolen by night Thus I was; in the day the drought consumed me, and the frost by night; and my sleep departed from mine eyes.

Thus have 1 been twenty years in thy house; I served thee fourteen years for thy two daughters, and six years for thy cattle: and thou hast changed my wages ten times.

Except the God of my father, the God of Abraham, and the fear of Isaac, had been with me, surely thou hadst sent me away now empty. God hath seen mine affliction and the labour of my hands, and rebuked thee yesternight. **Genesis 31:36-42**

There is a real progression in Jacob. God did beyond the prayers he made when he set out on his journey. Jacob served with Laban for twenty years. He did not run away or elope with Rachael.

When he was deceived into marrying the elder sister, he served another six years. For the animals, he had no fix wages but he stayed put. God answered his prayers and imparted godliness into him during those challenging twenty years; the climax of God's dealing was when he wrestled an angel at Jabbok, before confronting the ghost of his past, when he met Esau. He knew he could not receive the blessing, without transformation. God is more interested in your character than your comfort.

God is not interested in the voice of Jacob and hands of Esau blessings. So-called increases that come through sharp practices and underhandedness are not genuine. The Lord had to take Jacob through other severe tests that ensured his character was under guarding his faith. The fruit or character of Christ, needs time to grow. That is why we, sometimes, have repeated challenges in certain areas, on our way to receiving the blessings of God and, the greater purposes for our lives.

CHAPTER SIX

PERSECUTION

Nowadays believers don't want the world to laugh at them. We try to ensure that the world is not offended by the gospel we preach and our lifestyle. We know that an eagle caged in the company of parrots aborts its own destiny.

The believer is designed for distinction manifesting the glory of God. Like the eagle we are created to ride the storms of life to be distinct. We have a real enemy the devil he hates us with a passion. The believer who chooses to sit on the fence is actually agreeing with the devil. We are not called to be obnoxious or nasty to the unsaved but if we lie as the salt and the light of the world to which we are called then persecution must come.

But the God of all grace, who hath called us unto his eternal glory by Christ Jesus, after that ye have suffered a while, make you perfect establish strengthen settle you.
1 Peter 5:10

But and if ye suffer for righteousness' sake, happy are ye: and be not afraid of their terror, neither be troubled.
1 Peter 3:14

For it is better, if the will of God be so that ye suffer for well doing than for evil doing.
1 Peter 3:17

But let none of you suffer as a murderer, or as a thief, or as an evildoer, or as a busybody in other men's matters.
1 Peter 4:15

Yet if any man suffer as a Christian, let him not be ashamed but let him glorify God on this behalf. **1 Peter 4:16**

Wherefore let them that suffer according to the will of God commit the keeping of their souls to him in well doing, as unto a faithful Creator. **1 Peter 4:19**

And these are they likewise which are sown on stony ground; who, when they have heard the word, immediately receive it with gladness; And have no root in themselves, and so endure but for a time: afterward, when affliction or persecution ariseth for the word's sake, immediately they are offended. **Mark4:16-17**

Persecuted for word sake
The Lord Jesus made it clear that when the word is received, persecution will come because, the devil wants to challenge that word in the believer's life. It is instructive that Jesus said that, this person has no root but was really

excited, the time the word came to them. A plant with no root has not really blended with the environment.

This refers to people who see the life of faith as, a fad, or a get rich quick scheme. They are always listening for something that will happen fast. It is not a lifestyle some people think to follow Jesus as long as it would not change their life style, they can do all the things they know to be wrong but follow this five steps to success.

Root comes with commitment to the soil, it is character, giving when, your business is not going well. Fulfilling your commitment to tithe to the local church when things are a bit slow.

Walking in love when everybody is ugly at work. What the above scripture is saying is, opposition will come and if you are not committed, you will quit; this is not a quick weight loss program, it is a lifestyle that is uncompromising.

Don't try the word. Do it, don't start confessing, meditating, on the word, at the same time, planning your funeral. Attitude is the same as a trial marriage where you quit when it suits you. No root no commitment.

Being offended also means, when the answer is not quick in coming, and you gave a large amount and gave God time in which, he must meet your need. The date passes and you are mad at the Pastor and God. The first thing to check is your motive and secondly your commitment to the word.

Persecution for Godliness

Yea, and all that will live godly in Christ Jesus shall suffer persecution.
2Timothy3:12

By faith Moses, when he was come to years, refused to be called the son of Pharaoh's daughter; Choosing rather to suffer affliction with the people of God, than to enjoy the pleasures of sin for a season; Esteeming the

reproach of Christ greater riches than the treasures in Egypt: for he had respect unto the recompense of the reward. By faith he forsook Egypt, not fearing the wrath of the king: for he endured as seeing him who is invisible.
Hebrews 11:24-27

The Bible says that all that want to live to please God will suffer persecution. This means in your daily life people will mock you and speak against you. If nobody is persecuting you watch out.

There was a time in the church, where people imposed persecution on themselves. I still remember people who won't use the same bathroom with the unsaved, that won't shake hands with a female because of sanctification.

Many have since learned that, this is segregation not separation from the world. Jesus said we are in this world but not of it, we do not participate in the sinful things of the world. There is however another equally disturbing development some believers are trying to appeal to the world so much that we copy them. We get so close to sin that we are no longer bothered.

Some believers try to be so much like the world, trying to make Christianity un-offensive but forgetting that, Jesus said the world will hate us if we love him.

Moses was ready to pay the price by, leaving the pleasures of Egypt and the palace of the king and being identified with God's purpose. The reproach of Christ is the persecution and affliction that comes because of our faith.

It is true that you cannot clean a fish until it is caught but it is equally true that you cannot eat a fish that is not clean. Believers must be discipled to realize that, after salvation, there is a progressive journey to maturity.

Every church service cannot be a celebration meeting. There is a new generation of believers who, are not prepared for the reality and, hazards of the way. They are taught not to expect any challenges, when they come under attack, they fall by the way side.

This is a real journey there is celebration but the hazards are real. A church is not a fast food restaurant it is a home. While you were growing up, you did not like everything your mother served but like in my house, you ate them.

For the challenges ahead, we must expect persecution as we look to the coming of the Lord Jesus and, believers must know that, they must be willing to suffer for their positions. On social issues, the Bible is clear about losing certain privileges as Moses did.

CHAPTER SEVEN

FAITH UNDER FIRE

Training for the Olympics, athletes are busy for several years before their events, they change diets, travel to new location, give up certain pleasures, leave their families to win a gold medal etc.

The walk of faith can be likened to a relay race. We are supposed to pick up our batons individually and collectively and run where others left off.

God is expecting more dedication not less from the body of believers today because we have so much given to us. Our dedication must rise above the challenges of our day. Someone said the best way to kill a frog is to put it in a pan with water, and slowly heat the water.

As it gets comfortable it would die in the process. Christianity of comfort that calls for no sacrifice is the best way to loose the race. God's power is released to the level of dedication and the price we are willing to pay. No matter how long we live here it is only a preparation for eternity.

And they departed from the presence of the council, rejoicing that they were counted worthy to suffer shame for his name.
Acts 5:41

There are nations on the earth, where people are still paying the supreme price for their faith. I have known many who have paid this sort of price I have also known many who through their faith quenched the fury of certain death. To me, they are all precious people of faith. I share this to help others see that; people's faith in the kingdom is under fire in different situations. Someone is standing for their convictions in the work place, another is standing for his life on a street corner.

I remember the incidence of a woman in our congregation whose house, was surrounded by men who were killing and maiming Christians in her neighbourhood. They burned down homes next to hers and took the people's lives but, she stood firm declaring that she was redeemed from destruction.

She kept confessing that Jesus had paid for her life and she and her family owed the devil nothing. According to her testimony, they stared hard at her. There seemed to be something standing between them, and her. They could not come near the family so, they moved to the next house and continued the mayhem.

Another young man walked through a mob

while they were busy, hacking down an innocent man. He kept the word about the blood of Jesus. Redeeming his life from destruction in his mouth and they did not see him as he walked past.

According to his testimony, he was scared but the Lord reminded him that, he attended the communion midweek service and already declared that, the blood of Jesus on the mercy seat in heaven, was speaking redemption for him.

With that in mind, he walked through the mob. We received several testimonies like these, of angelic deliverances. A young executive, several years prior to this incident in the early years of our church, was accosted and told to deny his faith, his companion, was able to escape but he, stood firm and paid the supreme price. He died in faith.

Faith is not a fad, without commitment and character faith will fail. In the world of sports, a team under the threat of losing a game must show character.

The Apostle Paul and the early church best exemplify this: their commitment was total. Paul was stoned; given up for dead but surprisingly got up and went into the same city.

And there came thither certain Jews from Antioch and Iconium, who persuaded the people, and, having stoned Paul, drew him out of the city, supposing he had been dead Howbeit, as the disciples stood round about him, herose up and came into the city: and the next day he departed with Barnabas to Derbe. **Acts 14:19-20**

The early church leaders were flogged and warned not to preach in that name but they were out again, ministering. Their commitment was total.

The secret of Paul's life is that he did not count his life dear. In this age, this could mean that you do not consider anything in this material realm important enough, to deter you from your mission. Beatings, imprisonment, betrayals, burden of the churches, personal attacks did not affect Paul.

When you and I begin to look at the persecutions we face in the light of Paul's, we need to be encouraged that if the grace of God was sufficient for Paul, it would be more than sufficient for us.

I know a woman who has been in and out of jail on account of her faith, divorced and disinherited on account of her faith, no access to the basic conveniences of life but you never met a more joyful person.

The apostle Paul by the peculiar nature of his calling faced persecution everywhere he went, he faced them with courage and consolation in God. When we consider some of the challenges that we face and that of Paul and others we know that if God brought them through he will also deliver us. In the difficult times believers are tempted to quit but we must remember that this is a marathon.

You can always take consolation when persecuted for righteousness sake that the devil does not fight flops. The star player in a competitive game is always the centre of attraction: Depending on how vicious the opponents are, they might conspire to injure him and take him out of the game.

No wonder the Bible says the righteous has a lot of troubles but the Lord delivers him from them all. The psalmist also says when we are delivered we shall be honoured.

Many are the afflictions of the righteous: but the LORD deliverefh him out of them all.
Psalm 34:19

He shall call upon me, and I will answer him: I will be with him in trouble; I will deliver him, and honour him. **Psalm 91:15**

When there are no challenges no persecutions the believer needs to wonder if he still in the faith. If you give the devil the most trouble he will try to trip or upset you.

Paul had so much problems and challenges that I suppose in modern times because of the one sided view we take on faith some would consider that he had missed God.

Literarily everywhere Paul went the devil made trouble for him. Satan knows a man like Paul not chained will wreak havoc to his kingdom. When Paul woke up in the morning hell trembled and had an emergency session on what to do to stop the human bulldozer called Paul.

This is the reason they troubled him. In this day some translate small or no challenges to mean great faith in operation it can also mean nothing is happening.

Let us read some of what Paul had to say about

his challenges:

Of the Jews five times received I forty stripes save one. Thrice was I beaten with rods once was I stoned thrice I suffered shipwreck a night and a day I have been in the deep; In journeyings often, in perils of waters, in perils of robbers, in perils by mine own countrymen, in perils by the heathen, in perils in the city, in perils in the wilderness, in perils in the sea, in perils among false brethren; In weariness and painfulness, in watchings often, in hunger and thirst in fastings often, in cold and nakedness. Beside those things that are without, that which cometh upon me daily, the care of all the churches. Who is weak and I am not weak who is offended and I burn not? If I must needs glory I will glory of the things which concern mine infirmities.   **2 Corinthians 11:24-30**

Blessed be God, even the Father of our Lord Jesus Christ, the Father of mercies, and the God of all comfort; Who comforteth us in all our tribulation, that we may be able to comfort them which are in any trouble, by the comfort wherewith we ourselves are comforted of God. For as the sufferings of Christ abound in us, so our consolation also aboundeth by Christ. And whether we be afflicted it is for your consolation and salvation, which is effectual in the enduring of the same sufferings which we also suffer or whether we be comforted it is for your consolation and salvation. And our hope of you is steadfast, knowing that as ye are partakers of the sufferings, so shall ye be also of the consolation. For we would not, brethren, have you ignorant of our trouble which came to us in Asia, that we were pressed out of measure, above strength, insomuch that we despaired even of life. But we had the sentence of death in ourselves, that we should not trust in ourselves but in God which raiseth the dead: Who delivered us from so great a death, and doth deliver in whom we trust that he will yet deliver us.

2 Corinthians 1:3-10

You may not have ever experienced similar

situations like Paul; you have however, had a trying situation where you felt that If God did not come through for you, then all hope was gone. Imagine the most desperate situation in your life.

If you were trusting God for deliverance, you realized that your faith was also under fire because, you were under so much pressure, you drew closer to the Lord just as Paul said, you chose not to trust in yourself, but in God who raises the dead.

When Abraham was told to sacrifice Isaac, the Bible says, he believed that God could raise Isaac from the dead. No short cut, no tricks, the Lord's instruction was clear, sacrifice the boy. But, as he lifted his hands, he was totally submitted.

His trust was not in any man not even, in himself but in God who raises the dead. He reasoned that if God quickened the dead womb of Sarah, and his own body, when he had

Isaac, all he could do was lean on him only. At the time, he had Ishmael his body was still potent but by the time he had Isaac at ninety-nine years of age his body was dead.

When afflictions and persecutions that seems to be life threatening come they do one thing: they teach us not to trust in ourselves. We deepen our commitment, and God justifies us. After Abraham's obedience God commended Abraham saying, he knew Abraham's devotion.

But we had the sentence of death in ourselves, that we should not trust in ourselves but in God which raiseth the dead.
2 Corinthians 1:9

The blessing of total dependency on God is that your character develops at the expense of the devil. Satan sends all the problems to destroy your faith but God takes the same thing meant to destroy you and uses it for your advantage. When you meet a believer who has allowed the Holy Spirit to use the challenges the enemy has thrown at them to develop them they emit the fragrance of heaven like a cake properly baked.

You want to be near them because there is a good aroma. These are the living sacrifices the Bible talks about. An ornamental fruit plate filled with oranges, mangoes, bananas and other fruit is no use to a hungry man.

This is why Jesus insisted that men would know us by the fruit in our lives. In every area of faith God insists on our character being developed. We may get by for a little while without real character roots coming up but not for long.

Those who resist the Holy Spirit in this area end up faking things and are shipwrecked. You cannot fake the fruit of the spirit.

The world is hungry for reality. We believers as living epistles are not supposed to be like the fig tree that had leaves without fruit. Our attractiveness should not be for a fanciful attraction, but when people come in touch with us there must be real fruit we must have something real to give those who are hungry.

You cannot be a witness to something that is not real to you. God's intention is that we are not only talking the talk. We are required to walk the walk, the process is bearing the fruit of the spirit.

OTHER BOOKS BY DR TUNDE BOLANTA

- Answering the Call to the Ministry
- (available In Danish)
- Insecurity in Ministry
- Communion and the New Covenant
- Fear Not
- Everyday Promises of Jesus
- Anointing For Endurance
- Flies in the Ointment
- Discerning Ditches in the Last Days
- Seven Benefits of Righteousness
- Vessel Unto Honour
- Sex Fantasy and Reality
- Absent Without Leave
- Mentoring in Life & Ministry
- Understanding Seasons in Life & Ministry